Henry's mother and father had eight children, and Henry was the eighth of these. He was the last child in his family.

Parents usually spoil their youngest child. But Henry was not happy, because he was always the last at everything. He was always the last out of bed. He was always the last at the breakfast table. His brothers and sisters all laughed at him.

'You're a dreamer, Henry!' they said. 'You're always last!'

Henry was small and thin. The other children in his village did not like to play with him. They ran away from him. They shouted at him, 'Run, Henry, run! You can't catch us. You'll be last again!'

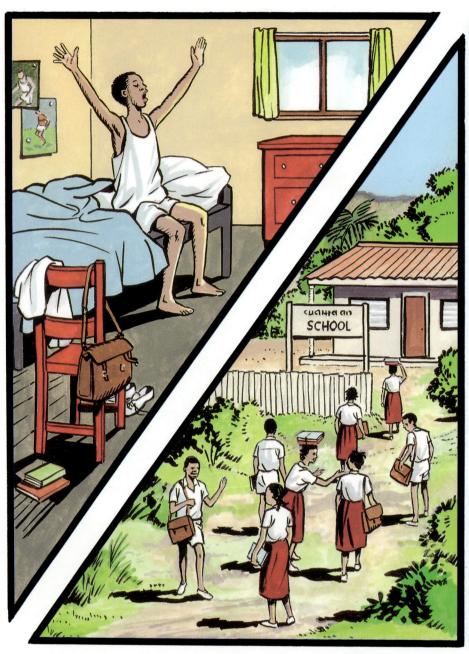

Henry did not like school. The school was a long way from his house. His friends left home early in the morning and walked to school. Henry was always the last out of the house.

His mother pushed him out of the house. She shouted after him, 'Run, Henry, run! You're late for school! Run, or you'll be last again.'

So Henry always ran to school. But he was always the last there. He was usually late.

Henry's teacher got angry. 'You were late again,' she said, 'so you must stay at school late, too. You're always the last at school, so you will go home last, too. We'll call you **Henry the Last**!'

So Henry was usually the last out of school. He always ran home after the other children. He ran like a gazelle, but he usually reached his village last.

When he left school, Henry found work in a town. The people in his family were good at making things. They made leather bags, belts and sandals. They made jewellery with beads and metal. They made beautiful clothes. Henry took a lot of these things to town with him. He sold them to people on the street. A lot of young men sold things on the street in the same way. Henry made friends with them.

But the police did not like street traders. They chased them and took away their things. Once they caught Henry and took away his things too. They sent him back to his village. But Henry got more things from his family, and he went back to the town again.

Whenever Henry's friends saw a police car, they jumped up, picked up their things and ran away as fast as they could. They used to shout to Henry, 'Run, Henry, run! Run, or you'll be caught again!'

Henry was usually dreaming. When the police came, everyone jumped up and ran away. He was always the last on his feet. But, by now, he could run like a hare. The police never caught him again.

When he was older, Henry joined the army. But he was not a good soldier. He liked to dream too much. He liked to lie in bed in the morning. He was always the last out of bed, the last at breakfast, the last on the parade ground.

Henry's sergeant always got angry. He used to shout at Henry, 'Run, run! You're last again!'

At the end of the day, the other soldiers went to dinner, but the sergeant called Henry back.

'You got here last,' he said, 'so now you can leave here last.'

He told Henry to run round and round the parade ground. 'Run, soldier, run!' he shouted. 'Run, and don't be last again!'

This happened very often.

Henry's sergeant was good at running. He wanted his soldiers to be good runners, too.

'Soldiers must run fast,' he said. 'They must be fit.'

One day the sergeant ran up into the hills. 'Follow me!' he shouted to his soldiers.

The sergeant ran uphill very fast. His soldiers followed him, but most of them could not run as fast as he could. Only Henry could keep up with his sergeant. By now, Henry was a very good runner.

Henry's sergeant was pleased. He said, 'Henry the Last, you can run very fast!'

The sergeant laughed, and all his soldiers laughed with him.

'Where did you learn to run like that?' they asked Henry.

'At school,' Henry answered. 'And I've done a lot of running in my life.'

A few weeks later, Henry ran in a big cross-country race. It was the Army Championships. There were hundreds of runners in the race. They ran for ten kilometres up and down the hills.

Henry started at the back. After the first kilometre, he was nearly last. He was dreaming about the hills near his home.

But then he heard some soldier friends shouting, 'Run, Henry, run! Run, or you'll be last again.'

By now, Henry did not like being last all the time.

'Run, Henry, run!' he said to himself. 'Run fast, and you'll be first this time!'

So he began to run faster and faster.

After five kilometres, there were only twenty runners in front of him.

After nine kilometres, there were only three. One of them was his sergeant.

'I can catch him,' Henry said to himself. 'I can run as fast as he can.'

Then he saw the finishing line in front of him. There were crowds of people there. By now, his sergeant was the only runner in front of him — just a few metres in front. Henry began to run as fast as he could. His soldier friends began to cheer for him, 'Run, Henry, run! Run fast, and you'll be first!'

But the sergeant heard Henry behind him. He turned his head and said, 'Henry the Last! You can't be first! You can't catch me!'

Then the sergeant ran like a lion. Henry could not catch him. Or perhaps he did not want to make his sergeant angry.

A few years later, Henry was running in the Olympic Games — in the final of the 10,000 metres. This time, he started at the front. By now, he liked to be first. He wanted a gold medal.

All round the track, thousands of people were cheering for him. All round the world, millions of people were watching him on television. Back at home, his friends and family were cheering for him, too.

'Run, Henry, run!' shouted his old friends from the village. 'Run fast, or you'll be last again!'

After one kilometre, Henry was twenty metres in front of the other runners.

'Run, Henry, run!' shouted his family and friends. 'Run fast, and you'll be first again!'

'Not too fast!' shouted his old sergeant. 'Don't go too fast, or you won't win.'

After nine kilometres, he was a hundred metres in front, but he was feeling very tired. The other runners were catching him fast. He felt that he was running in a dream.

'Run, Henry, run!' shouted his old friends from the town. 'Run fast, or you'll be caught again!'

Then Henry heard a bell. It rang loud in his ear. It was the bell for the last lap, but it sounded like the bell at his old school. In a dream, he heard his mother's voice again, 'Run, Henry, run! You're late for school. Run, or you'll be last again!'

In a dream, he heard his teacher saying, 'We'll call you **Henry the Last**!'

Henry did not want to be last any more. He wanted to be first — always first! He woke up and ran like the wind.

A few minutes later, he was standing on a box with a medal round his neck. It was a gold medal.

'Henry,' his team manager said. 'You finished first. But that's not all. You also broke the world record for 10,000 metres. Now you are the first in the world!'

Since that day, his friends call him **Henry the First**.

HOP STEP JUMP

In My Father's Village   Michael Palmer
Striped Paint   Rosina Umelo
The Slow Chameleon and Shammy's Bride   David Cobb
The Walking Talking Flying ABC   David Cobb
Raindrops In Africa   Margaret House
Sing It, Do It   David Cobb
No Problem!   Rosina Umelo
Ten Ripe Mangoes   David Cobb
The Best Bed In The World   Charlotte Mbali
Under The Cotton Tree   David Cobb
Lucky Day!   Lynn Kramer

Choose Me!   Lynn Kramer
Nondo The Cow   Diane Rasteiro
Sika In The Snow   David Cobb
Henry The Last   Michael Palmer
My Life On The Wing   David Cobb
The Radio Thief   Anthony K Johnson
The Grasshopper War   Thokozile Chaane
The Numberheads   Robyn Roberts
The All-Day Dreamer   Karen W Mbugua and Geoff Baier
Honeybrown And The Bees   Jill Inyundo
Lissa's Rainbow Dress   Joyce Ama Addo
The Bug Collector   Gillian Leggat
A Job On The Moon   Michael Montgomery
The Lily Pool   Jill Inyundo
Want To Be A Strongman?   Michael Montgomery
The Cowrie Seekers   Shelley Davidow
Ibuka And The Lost Children   Sibylla Martin

Chichi And The Termites   Wendy Ijioma
The Boy Who Ate A Hyena   James G D Ngumy
Tickets For The Zed Band   Lynn Kramer
Knife Boy   Michael Montgomery
Chichi's Nature Diary   Wendy Ijioma
Fair Shares   Lynn Kramer
Paa Bena And The New Canoe   Phyllis Addy
Chimpanzee Rescue   Margaret House
The Calabash And The Box   Bobson Sesay
Check, Come Here!   Edison Yongai
You Can't Grow Footballs From Seeds   Margaret Spencer
Pepi Mazamban, Mender of Cars, Age 10   James Mason
Water Girl   Michael Montgomery
Two Eggs For The President   Marianna Brandt
Search For The Stone Bird   Shelley Davidow

POETRY
On The Poetry Bus   ed. David Cobb
Sometimes When It Rains   Achirri Chi-Bikom
Riding A Rainbow   Achirri Chi-Bikom